Transcribed by Ola Gjeilo & Federico Incitti
Edited by James Welland & Ola Gjeilo
Music typesetting by Sam Lung

ISBN 978-1-5400-9036-2

CHESTER MUSIC
part of **WiseMusic**Group

EXCLUSIVELY DISTRIBUTED BY
HAL•LEONARD®

Visit Hal Leonard Online at
www.halleonard.com

Contact us:
Hal Leonard
7777 West Bluemound Road
Milwaukee, WI 53213
Email: info@halleonard.com

In Europe, contact:
Hal Leonard Europe Limited
42 Wigmore Street
Marylebone, London, W1U 2RN
Email: info@halleonardeurope.com

In Australia, contact:
Hal Leonard Australia Pty. Ltd.
4 Lentara Court
Cheltenham, Victoria, 3192 Australia
Email: info@halleonard.com.au

PREFACE

I love nighttime. I love the mood of night, and feeling all of New York City light up
from endless skyscrapers. There's something very inspiring and even reassuring
and calming about that to me. New York at night is very romantic, I think.

So, all the pieces on this album were created in the evening; I did several
recording sessions at studios all over the city - free improvisations, some of which
would later turn into these tracks. And it was so fun, I love working that way; just being
completely open and directionless and not let my thoughts get in the way, until
I eventually can edit, rework and shape them into coherent pieces.

What I wanted with this album was to create tracks that were short,
transparent and heartfelt expressions of my deep affection and
gratitude for the city I love and get to call home.

Ola Gjeilo

CONTENTS

FIREFLY

Ola Gjeilo

STILL

Ola Gjeilo

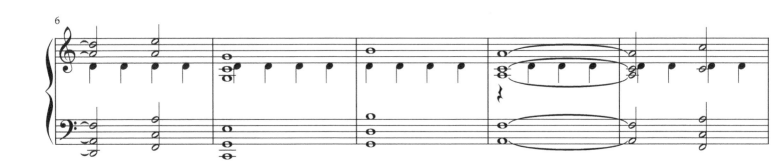

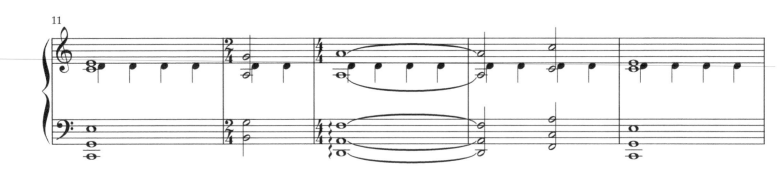

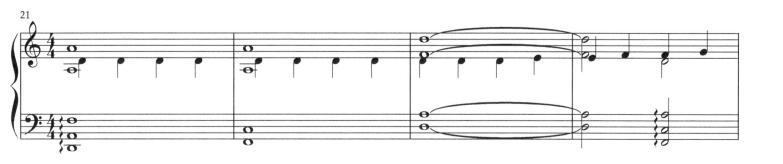

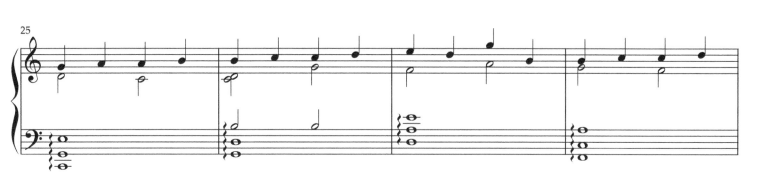

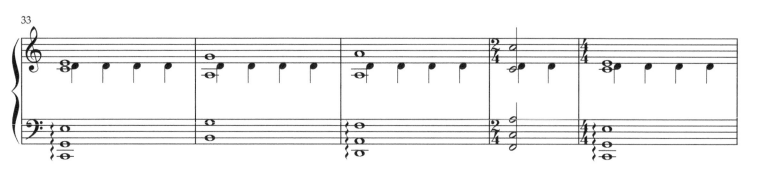

poco rit. _ _ _ _

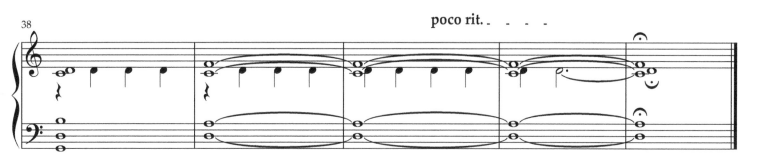

SLEEPLESS

Ola Gjeilo

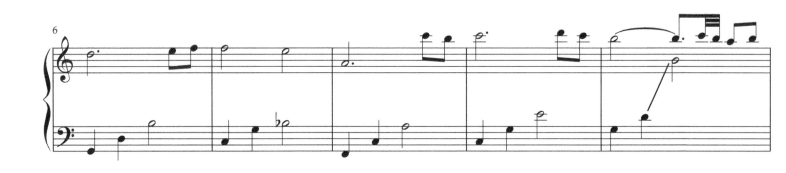

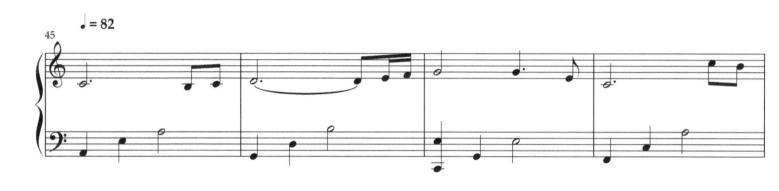

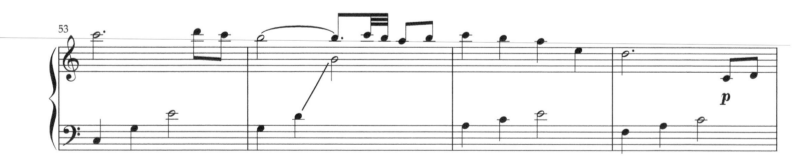

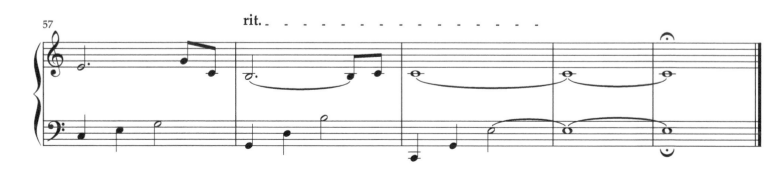

CITY LIGHTS

Ola Gjeilo

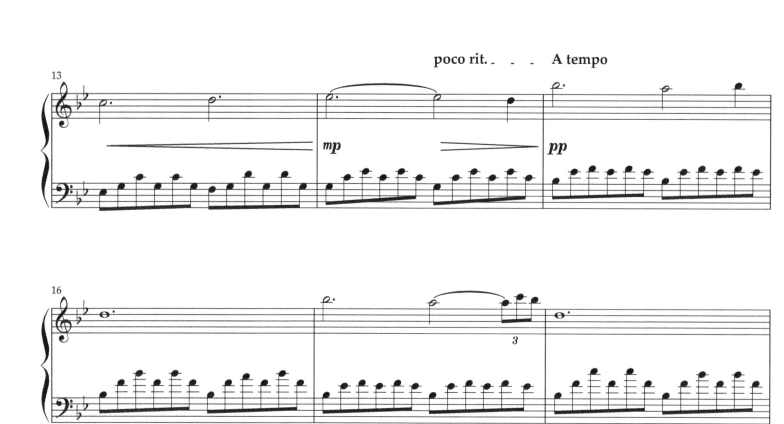

poco rit. _ _ _   A tempo

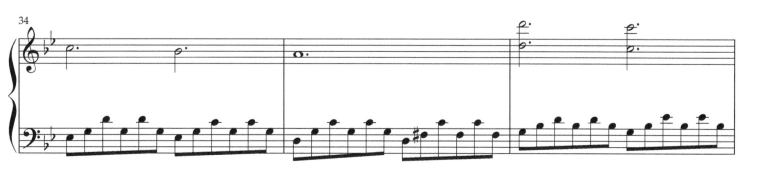

rit. _ _ _ _ _ _ _ _ _ _ _

NIGHT RAIN

Ola Gjeilo

poco rit.

A tempo

p

poco rit.   A tempo

pp

poco rit.   A tempo

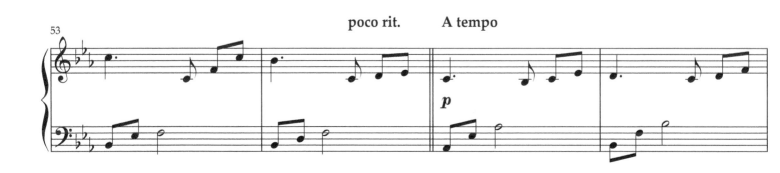

p

poco rit.   A tempo

poco rit.

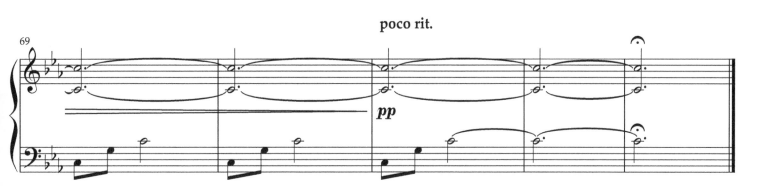

BEFORE DAWN

Ola Gjeilo

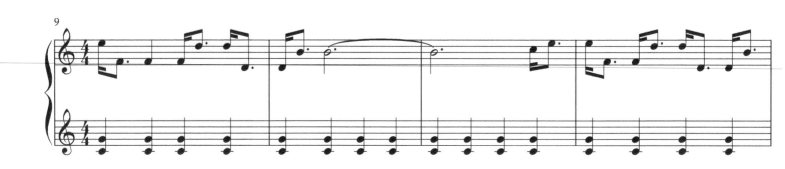

19

FIREFLY

Ola Gjeilo

CONTENTS

AEON

Ola Gjeilo

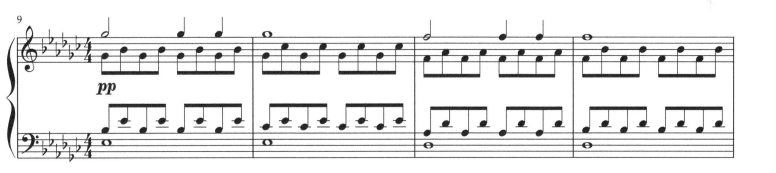

rit. - - -

A tempo

CRYSTAL SKY

Ola Gjeilo

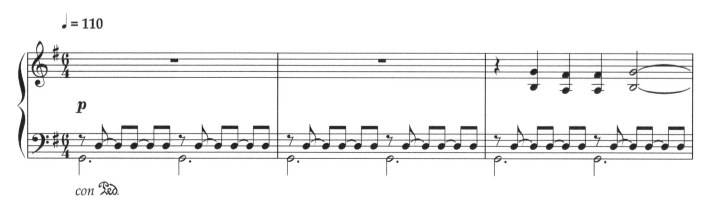

QUIET STREETS

Ola Gjeilo

29

SUNDOWN

Ola Gjeilo

poco rit. _ _ _

MOONRISE

Ola Gjeilo

♩. = 96

pp

con Ped., una corda

rit. _ _ _ _ _ _ _ _ _

A tempo

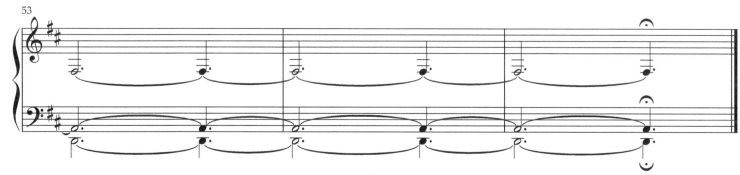

34

SHADOWS

Ola Gjeilo

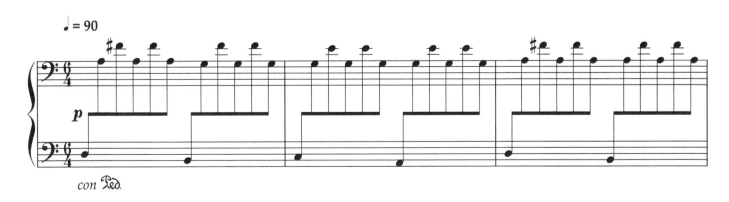

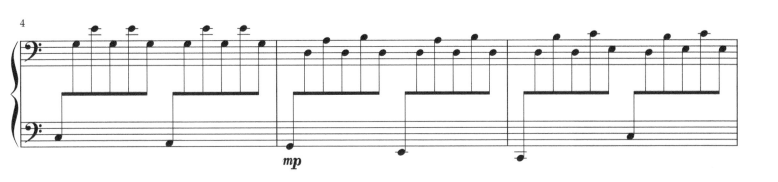

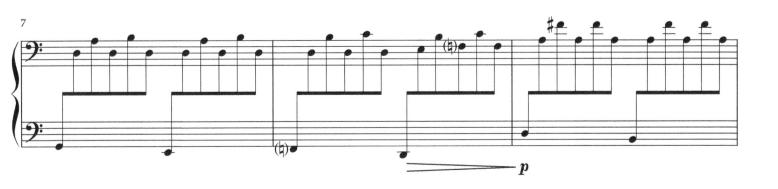

A tempo

poco rit. _ _ _   A tempo

rit. _ _ _ _

A tempo

poco rit. . _ _ _ A tempo

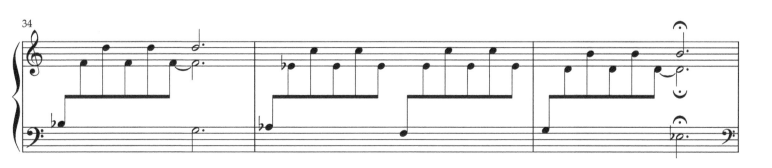

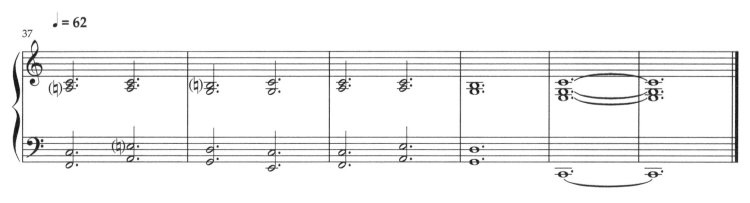

ECLIPSE

Ola Gjeilo

poco rit. _ _ _ _ _ _ _ _ _

AURORA

Ola Gjeilo

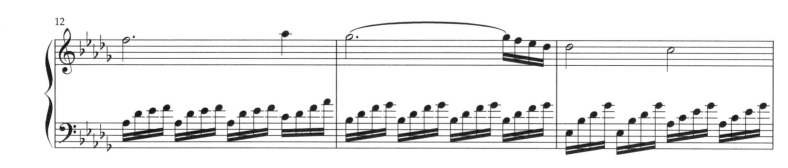

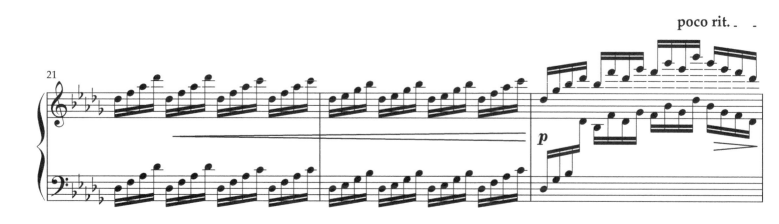

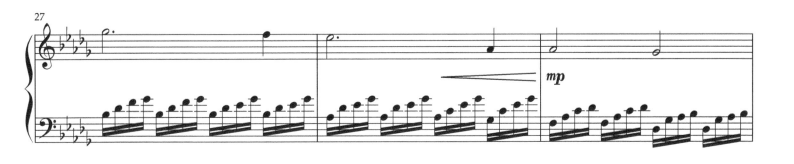

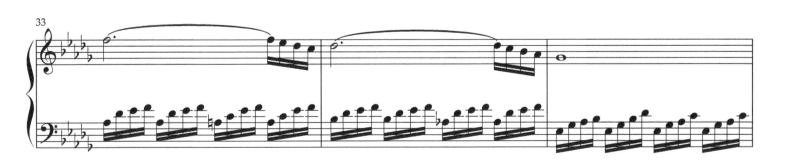

DREAMING

Ola Gjeilo

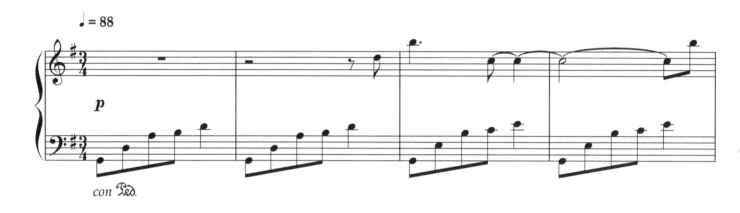

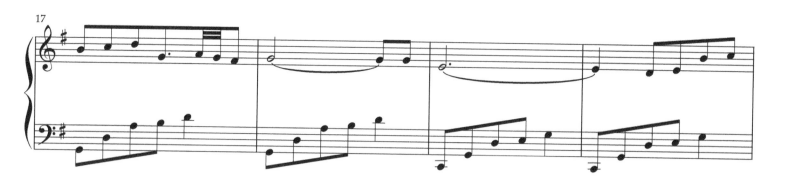

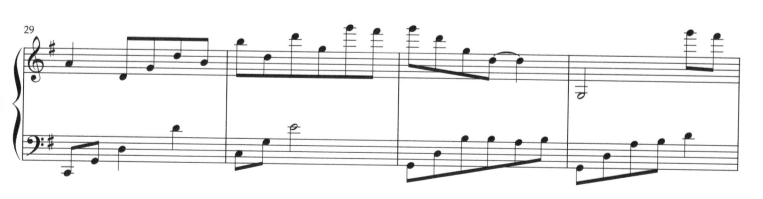

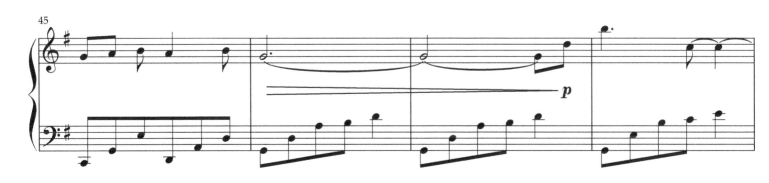

poco rit. - - - - - - -

pp

POLAR

Ola Gjeilo

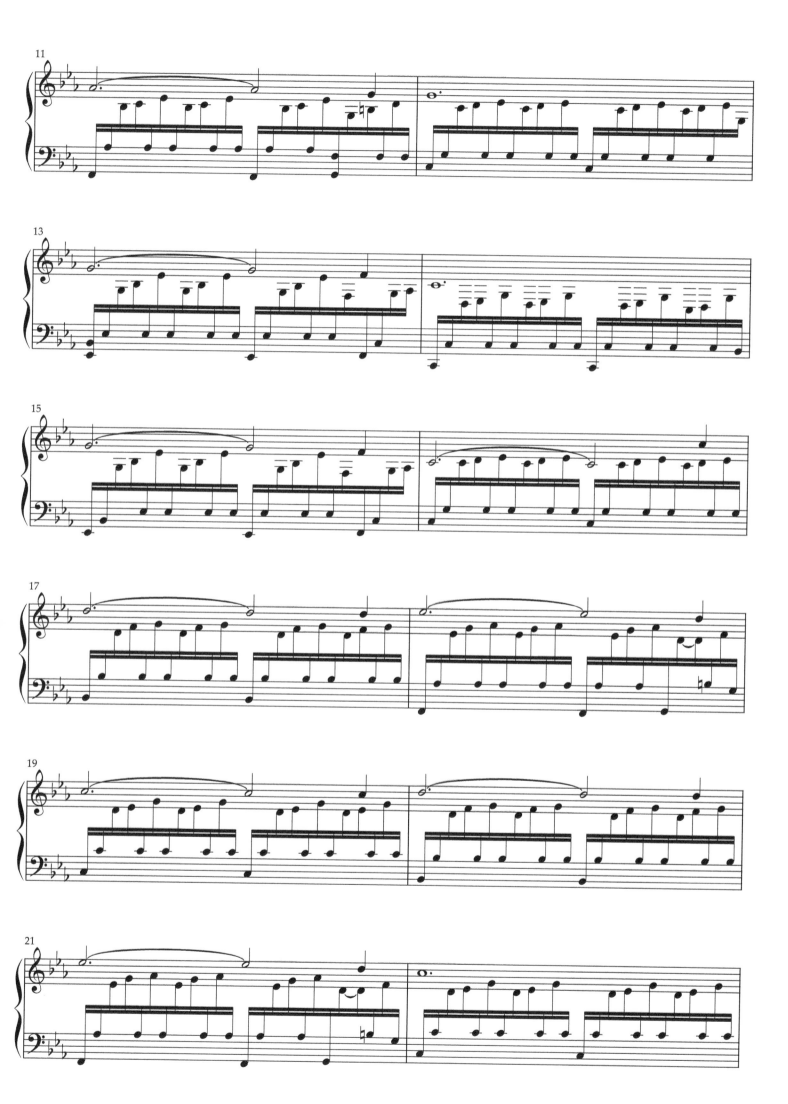

SKYLINE

Ola Gjeilo

NOCTURNAL

Ola Gjeilo

rit. _ _ _ _ _ _ _